New York in the New Nation

James Bernard

New York

Published in 2015 by The Rosen Publishing Group, Inc.
29 East 21st Street, New York, NY 10010

Book Design: Chris Brand

Photo Credits: Cover Interim Archives/Archive Photos/Getty Images; pp. 5, 17 (both), 19 (inset), 21 (both) © Bettman/Corbis; p. 7 (inset) © Hulton/Archive; pp. 7, 19 © New York State Archives; p. 9 Fotosearch/Stringer/Archive Photos/ Getty Images; p. 11 (inset) Ben Hider/Getty Images Entertainment/Getty Images; p. 11 Stock Montage/Archive Photos/Getty Images; p. 13 (top) © New York Public Library; p. 13 (bottom) Library of Congress Prints and Photographs Division Washington, D.C.; p. 15 (inset) Universal History Archive/Universal Images Group/ Getty Images; p. 15 DEA Picture Library/De Agostini/Getty Images.

Library of Congress Cataloging-in-Publication Data

Bernard, James.
New York in the new nation / by James Bernard.
p. cm. — (Spotlight on New York)
Includes index.
ISBN 978-1-4777-7343-7 (pbk.)
ISBN 978-1-4777-7282-9 (6-pack)
ISBN 978-1-4777-7318-5 (library binding)
1. New York (State)—History—1775–1865—Juvenile literature. I. Bernard, James. II. Title.
F122.B47 2015
974.7—d23

Manufactured in the United States of America

CPSIA Compliance Information: Batch #WS15RC: For further information contact Rosen Publishing, New York, New York at 1-800-237-9932.

Contents

The American Revolution

From 1664 to 1776, New York was a British **colony**. By the 1770s, some colonists wanted to be free from English rule. They called themselves **patriots**. Other colonists stayed loyal to Britain's king. They were called **loyalists**. Sometimes there were patriots and loyalists in the same family, which caused many disagreements and sometimes violence.

On April 23, 1775, a messenger arrived in New York City. He brought news from Boston that the patriots and the British had fought at Lexington and Concord, in Massachusetts. The **American Revolution** had begun! The colonists were fighting for their **independence** from Great Britain. On July 4, 1776, the Declaration of Independence was signed. Leaders in New York approved it five days later, on July 9. The British colonies had become independent states.

The British captured New York City soon after the Declaration of Independence was signed and controlled it for the next seven years. The Continental Army built a line of forts along the Hudson River to prevent the British from moving north. These forts helped keep the British from capturing the rest of New York.

The Declaration of Independence was read aloud to the public for the first time in New York City. The reading took place in the city's Commons, today's City Hall Park.

The First Constitution

On July 10, 1776, a convention of New York patriots met in White Plains, New York, to establish a **government** to replace the pro-British New York Assembly. After numerous meetings in various places, the delegates **adopted** New York's first **constitution** in Kingston, New York, on April 20, 1777.

The constitution created a legislative, or lawmaking, branch made up of two separate bodies, one called an assembly and one called a senate. On July 30, 1777, George Clinton became the first **governor** of New York. Clinton had been a general in the New York militia and the Continental Army.

In September 1783, the Treaty of Paris was signed, ending the American Revolution. The colonies won their independence from Great Britain. The new nation needed a government. Patriot leaders from the thirteen rebellious colonies created the Articles of Confederation, which was the nation's constitution from 1781 to 1789. The thirteen independent states became the United States.

The image in the back is New York's first state constitution. Along with the Articles of Confederation, seen in the inset, the state constitution helped establish law and order in New York State.

51. This Convention therefore in the Name & by th[e]
Authority of the Good People of this State, doth ordain deter[mine]
and declare that no Authority shall on any Pretence what[ever]
be exercised over the People or Members of this State, but s[uch]
as shall be derived from and Granted by them. ×

§3 And Whereas Laws inconsistant with the Spu[rit]
of this Constitution or with the publick Good may be
[has]tily & Unadvisedly passed; Be it Ordained that [the]
Governor for the Time being, the Chancellor & the Judg[es]
[a]ny two of them, together [with]
[the] hereby are Constituted [a]
[B]ills about to be passed [in]
And for that purpose sh[all]
[from] time to time when the [Legis]
[con]vened; for which neverth[eless]
[ha]ve any Sallary or Consi[deration]
[what]ever. And that a[ll]
[d] the Senate & Assemb[ly]
[Bi]lls Laws, be presented to th[e]
[re]visal & Consideration; an[d]
Consideration it should
[an]d Council, or a Majority
[al]l should become a law
[i]n the same together w[ith]
[the]re in Writing to the Sen[ate]
[the] same shall [have] originated

New York State and the US Constitution

Under the Articles of Confederation, the United States did not have a strong national government. It was hard to run a country without one, though. In 1786, **delegates** from five states met in Annapolis, Maryland, to discuss this problem. New York sent two delegates, Alexander Hamilton and Egbert Benson. The delegates decided that the Articles of Confederation needed to be changed.

In May 1787, delegates gathered in Philadelphia for a meeting called the Constitutional Convention. This time New York sent three delegates. Instead of changing the Articles of Confederation, the delegates wrote the US Constitution, a new set of rules by which the country would be governed. Nine states had to **ratify** the Constitution for it to take effect.

New Yorkers Alexander Hamilton and John Jay and Virginian James Madison wrote 85 essays promoting the ratification of the Constitution. The essays, most of which were published **anonymously** in New York newspapers, are now called the Federalist Papers. After much debate and a close vote, New York became the eleventh state to ratify the Constitution on July 26, 1788. Though the Constitution had become law by then, New York's support was seen as key to its long-term success.

THE

FEDERALIST:

A COLLECTION

OF

ESSAYS,

WRITTEN IN FAVOUR OF THE

NEW CONSTITUTION,

AS AGREED UPON BY THE FEDERAL CONVENTION,
SEPTEMBER 17, 1787.

IN TWO VOLUMES.

VOL. I.

NEW-YORK:

PRINTED AND SOLD BY J. AND A. McLEAN,
No. 41, HANOVER-SQUARE,
M,DCC,LXXXVIII,

Although they originally appeared in newspapers and journals, the essays that we now call the Federalist Papers were also collected and printed in two volumes. The title page of the first of these volumes is shown here.

A Growing State

New York State changed a lot after the Revolution. The state's borders were defined during this period. The land east of Lake Champlain became Vermont, the fourteenth state to join the Union. People moving through the Hudson and Mohawk Valleys into the western part of the state soon built farms and small communities there. Some of the Iroquois who sided with the British during the Revolution moved north into British Canada. The Iroquois who remained, most of whose land had been lost through questionable treaties and sales, today reside on eight **reservations** in the state. The Algonquian Stockbridge Indians settled near Utica but later moved to Wisconsin. The Shinnecocks and Poospatucks stayed on Long Island.

New York's cities were also busy and growing. Albany, the state capital, had started as a Dutch settlement over 250 years earlier. By this time, it was a center of transportation and industry, a gateway to the west, and a busy **port**. The city of Hudson, New York, was established in 1785 by merchants from Nantucket, Massachusetts. It was the first chartered city in the United States under the new American government. Buffalo was **founded** in 1803, and Rochester in 1812. Both cities began as small villages, Buffalo a center of trade and Rochester a center of farming.

The top picture shows Albany in 1828. As you can see, Albany was a large city even then. Boats of many sizes crowded the Hudson River in front of the city. The lower picture shows a main street in Albany in 1904. By the 1900s, Albany had already become a bustling supply center.

The Bank of New York

The Bank of New York was founded in June 1784. It is the oldest bank in the United States. Alexander Hamilton wrote the constitution that set up the Bank of New York. In 1789, President Washington appointed Hamilton the United States secretary of the Treasury. As the secretary of the Treasury, Hamilton was responsible for creating the economic **policies** of Washington's administration. He also played a key role in establishing the country's first national bank and the US Mint, which produced coins to replace the individual state **currencies** that were in use at the time.

Alexander Hamilton also played a role in the nation's trade. He opened trade with Great Britain, which many people still considered to be an enemy of the United States. Hamilton sent John Jay, the chief justice of the United States, to Great Britain to **negotiate**. In 1794, Jay arranged a treaty with Great Britain, which allowed the United States to trade with Great Britain and its colonies. This helped the American economy grow. Under the Jay Treaty, the British also surrendered several forts on American soil, including Fort Niagara, in western New York.

Two men who helped the economy of the young United States were Alexander Hamilton and John Jay. Hamilton created the Bank of New York and Jay's negotiations helped America gain the right to trade with the British Empire.

The Invention of the Steamboat

Inventors helped New York grow. Before the invention of the railroad, ships were used to carry goods and passengers from one place to another. These wind-powered ships were slow. When the steam engine was invented, people thought it could be used to make ships travel faster. Robert Fulton was an American **engineer** who was famous for his work with steam engines. He spent much of his life looking for newer and better ways to travel on **waterways**.

Although many of Fulton's early inventions didn't work, he did not give up. At the age of forty-two, he came up with a design for a steamboat. On August 17, 1807, his **steamboat**, the *North River,* sailed from New York City to Albany and back. It was the fastest trip between the two cities ever made. The steamboat was later renamed the *Clermont,* after the house of Robert Livingston, an important patriot during the American Revolution and the man who gave Fulton the money to build his steamboat. The *Clermont* made regular trips between the two cities. Fulton died at the age of fifty in New York City.

The *Clermont* took about thirty-two hours to travel from New York City to Albany. Before Fulton's invention, it took up to four days for a sailboat to make that same trip.

Robert Fulton

America's First National Waterway

Before there were any railroads, the only way to move large numbers of people or goods from one place to another was by water. Ships leaving New York Harbor could sail across the Atlantic Ocean to reach Europe and other parts of the world. However, it was difficult to transport goods from the country's **interior** to New York City. No waterway connected the city to the Great Lakes and the lands further west. DeWitt Clinton decided to change this.

Clinton was the mayor of New York City from 1803 to 1815. He was elected governor of New York State twice, serving from 1825 to 1828. In 1811, he supported plans for a **canal** that would connect the Hudson River to Lake Erie. It would be 363 miles long. Construction on the Erie Canal began in 1817 and was completed in 1825.

The Erie Canal led to the growth of cities along the canal such as Utica, Syracuse, Rochester, and Buffalo. It brought farm settlers westward and connected the Great Lakes to New York Harbor.

The document shown here announces a celebration for the opening of the Erie Canal. Before the canal was built, it cost more to ship goods thirty miles inland than it did to ship goods to England! The canal shortened the time it took for goods to travel from Buffalo to New York City from three weeks to about one week and cut the cost from $100 to about $10!

JULY 4, 1817.

OCTOBER 26, 1825.

Grand Celebration!

At a Meeting of the Committee of Arrangements appointed by the citizens of Geneva to make suitable arrangements for the celebration of the COMPLETION of the ERIE CANAL, and the Meeting of the Waters of the Great Western Lakes and the Atlantic Ocean, on WEDNESDAY the 26th instant, it was

Resolved, That, for the purpose of demonstrating the joy which the citizens of Geneva, in common with the citizens of the State, feel at the completion of the Erie Canal, it be recommended to them to partake of a Public DINNER, at the *Franklin House,* on Wednesday the 26th inst. at 4 o'clock P. M.

Resolved, That it be recommended to the Citizens of Geneva to ILLUMINATE their houses on the evening of the 26th instant.

Resolved, That a Public BALL be also recommended on the evening of the day on which the first Boat departing from Buffalo, on the Erie Canal, shall arrive at New York, at such place as the Managers shall designate; and that Nicholas Ayrault, Andrew P. Tillman, Wm. V. I. Mercer, L. B. Mizner, William W. Watson, John Smith, Jun. Hiram Walbridge, James Bogert, Charles A. Williamson, Andrew Burns, David S. Hall, George Stafford, Godfrey J. Grosvenor, and John T. Wilson, be Managers of said Ball.

A NATIONAL SALUTE will be fired by a detachment from Capt. Lu[...] ry Company, at twelve o'clock at noon: the bells will ring during the firing of [...]

The Illumination to commence at the ringing of the bells, about half pas[...] in the evening.

☞ Those citizens who wish to partake of the Dinner, are requested to [...] names at the Bookstore of J. Bogert, at the Reading Rooms, or at the Fran[...] by 10 o'clock to-morrow morning.

☞ Our Fellow-Citizens of the country generally, are invited to unite i[...] bration at this place.

ELNATHAN NOBLE,
CHARLES BUTLER,
WILLIAM W. WATSON,
HIRAM WALBRIDGE,
DAVID S. HALL,

ANDREW P. TILL[...]
JOHN SMITH, Jun.
CASTLE SOUTHE[...]
CHARLES LUM[...]
Committee of Arr[...]

GENEVA, Tuesday morning, October 25, 1825.

DeWitt Clinton

19

The Knickerbocker Group

Many of the nation's first famous writers and artists lived in New York City. In 1809, an **author** named Washington Irving published a book called *A History of New York* under the name Diedrich Knickerbocker. Knickerbocker is a Dutch name and Irving chose it to celebrate New York's Dutch history.

Today, the word "Knickerbocker" is used to describe any New Yorker. The word "Knickerbocker" is also used to describe a group of New York writers who wrote in and about New York in the early nineteenth century. These writers wanted to celebrate the region's history and culture. Together, the Knickerbocker Group created a **uniquely** American form of literature.

Irving's *A History of New York* became a bestseller. He followed it up with popular stories like "Rip Van Winkle" and "The Legend of Sleepy Hollow." James Fenimore Cooper was another New York writer. He wrote *The Last of the Mohicans*, a tale about settlers and Native Americans during the colonial wars. Other members of the Knickerbocker Group included James Kirke Paulding and William Cullen Bryant.

Washington Irving's story "Rip Van Winkle" was published in 1819. This 1849 painting, called *The Return of Rip Van Winkle*, is based on Irving's classic story.

Washington Irving

21

Diversity in New York

New York State has been home to **immigrants** since the first European settlers arrived in the early 1600s. The original Dutch settlers welcomed people from all over Europe to New Netherland. At one time, there were nineteen different languages being spoken in the Dutch colony. When the English took control of New Netherland in 1664, immigrants from across Europe continued to arrive.

In the twenty years after the American Revolution ended, the population of New York State almost tripled in size. Many of these settlers came from the New England states, moving into the western parts of New York that had once belonged to the Iroquois. Immigrants also continued to arrive from countries in Europe. German, Welsh, Scottish, and Irish immigrants helped cities like Utica, Syracuse, Buffalo, and Rochester grow and prosper. These immigrants brought farming and manufacturing skills that helped New York's economy grow.

Glossary

adopted: Accepted and put into effect.

American Revolution: The war that the American colonists fought from 1775 to 1783 to win independence from England.

anonymously: Without any name, such as author or contributor, mentioned.

author: A writer.

canal: A man-made waterway.

colony: A region settled by people from another land who keep their loyalty to their homeland.

Congress of the Confederation: The governing body of the United States of America that existed between 1781 and 1789.

constitution: A written set of rules by which a state or nation is governed.

currencies: Things that are used as money or a medium of exchange.

delegates: People chosen to represent a person or group of people.

engineer: A person trained to use scientific knowledge to solve practical problems.

founded: Set up or established.

government: A system of ruling a state, country, or community.

governor: One elected or appointed to manage a region.

immigrants: People who move to another country, usually for permanent residence.

independence: Freedom from control.

interior: The inland parts of a country or region.

loyalists: Colonists who supported Great Britain during the American Revolution.

negotiate: To deal or bargain with another or others.

patriots: The colonists in the Thirteen Colonies who rebelled against British control during the American Revolution.

policies: Plans developed by governments to guide decision making.

port: Place where people and merchandise can enter or leave a country.

ratify: To give formal approval.

reservations: Areas of land managed and governed by one or more Native American tribes.

steamboat: A boat propelled by a steam engine.

uniquely: In a singular or unusual fashion.

waterways: Natural or man-made rivers and canals that can be used to transport goods.

Index

Primary Source List

Page 7. *New York Constitution.* 1777. Now kept at the New York State Archives, Albany, NY.

Page 7 (inset). *Articles of Confederation.* 1777. Now in the National Archives and Records Administration, Washington, DC.

Page 9. *The Federalist.* Written by James Madison, Alexander Hamilton, and John Jay. Print. Compilation published by J. and A. McLean. 1788. Now kept at the Rare Books and Special Collections Division in the Library of Congress, Washington, DC.

Page 13 (top). *Albany, Capital of the State of New York.* Created by Jacques Gérard Milbert. Engraving. Printed in *Itinéraire Pittoresque du Fleuve Hudson et des parties latérales de l'Amérique du Nord.* 1828–1829. Copy of the engraving is now kept at the New York State Archives, Albany, NY.

Page 13 (bottom). *State Street and Capitol, Albany, NY.* Printed by Detroit Publishing Co. Photograph. 1904. Now kept at the Library of Congress Prints and Photographs Division, Washington, DC.

Page 15. *Alexander Hamilton.* Created by John Trumbull. Oil on canvas. 1806. Now kept at the George Washington University Law School, Washington, DC.

Page 15 (inset). *Portrait of John Jay.* Created by Gilbert Stuart. Oil on canvas. 1794. Now kept at the National Gallery of Art, Washington, DC.

Page 19. *"Grand Celebration!" Broadside announcing celebration to be held in Geneva, New York, in honor of the opening of the Erie Canal.* Print. 1825. Now kept at the New York State Archives, Albany, NY.

Page 19 (inset). *Portrait of Governor DeWitt Clinton.* Oil on canvas. Ca. 1800–1828. Now kept at the George F. Baker Houses, New York, NY.

Page 21. *The Return of Rip Van Winkle.* Created by John Quidor. Oil on canvas. 1849. Now kept at the National Gallery of Art, Washington, DC.

Page 21 (inset). *Washington Irving.* Created by Matthew Brady. Photograph. Ca. 1861. Now kept at the Library of Congress Prints and Photographs Division, Washington, DC.

Websites

Due to the changing nature of Internet links, Rosen Publishing has developed an online list of websites related to the subject of this book. This site is updated regularly. Please use this link to access the list: **http://www.rcbmlinks.com/nysh/nynn**